√

Pine Trees

by Marcia S. Freeman

Consulting Editor:
Gail Saunders-Smith, Ph.D.

Consultant:
Jeff Gillman, Associate Professor
of Nursery Management,
University of Minnesota

Pebble Books

an imprint of Capstone Press
Mankato, Minnesota

Pebble Books are published by Capstone Press
818 North Willow Street, Mankato, Minnesota 56001
http://www.capstone-press.com

Library of Congress Cataloging-in-Publication Data
Freeman, Marcia S. (Marcia Sheehan), 1937–
    Pine Trees/by Marcia S. Freeman.
    p. cm.—(Trees)
    Includes bibliographical references and index.
    Summary: Simple text and photographs describe the trunks, branches,
needles, and seeds of pine trees.
    ISBN 0-7368-0095-6
    1. Pine—Juvenile literature. [1. Pine. 2. Trees.] I. Title. II. Series: Trees
(Mankato, Minn.)
QK494.5.P66F741   1999
585'.2—dc21   98-22679
                                                        CIP
                                                        AC

Note to Parents and Teachers

Books in this series may be used together in comparative activities
to investigate different types of trees. This series supports national
science standards for the diversity and unity of plant life units.
This book describes and illustrates the parts of pine trees. The
photographs support early readers in understanding the text. This
book introduces early readers to vocabulary used in this subject
area. The vocabulary is defined in the Words to Know section. Early
readers may need assistance in reading some words and in using
the Table of Contents, Words to Know, Read More, Internet Sites,
and Index/Word List sections of the book.

Table of Contents

4

Pine trees grow to be big trees. They have straight trunks.

A pine tree has brown, black, or red bark. The bark is rough with small cracks.

8

Pine branches grow out from the trunk. Branches are long at the bottom of the tree. Branches are short at the top of the tree.

10

A pine tree has leaves called needles. Pine needles are thin and sharp. They can be long or short.

Pine needles grow on branches. Needles grow in groups of two, three, or five.

14

A pine tree has needles all year long. Pine trees are called evergreens.

16

A pine tree makes cones. Cones have woody parts called scales. Pine seeds are under the scales.

Pine seeds fall from cones. New pine trees grow from some seeds.

You can tell a pine tree
by its needles and cones.

Words to Know

bark—the hard covering on the outside of a tree

branch—a part of a tree that grows out of a tree's trunk

cone—the hard woody fruit on pine trees; cones hold pine seeds.

crack—a break or a narrow opening; the bark of some pine trees looks like it has cracks.

evergreen—a tree that has leaves throughout the year; pine trees have green needles all year long.

needle—a thin, pointed leaf on a pine tree

rough—having bumps and dents

scale—a small, thin plate; woody scales cover cones.

straight—not bent or curved

trunk—the main stem of a tree

Read More

Gamlin, Linda. *Trees.* Eyewitness Explorers. New York: Dorling Kindersley, 1993.

Oppenheim, Joanne. *Have You Seen Trees?* New York: Scholastic, 1995.

Pine, Jonathan. *Trees.* A HarperCollins Nature Study Book. New York: HarperCollins, 1995.

Internet Sites

Arbor Day Kids Home Page
http://www.arborday.net/kids

Pine Cone Identification
http://bluehen.ags.udel.edu/udbg/cones.html

Western White Pine
http://www.zip.com.au/~elanora/tusidaho.html

Index/Word List

bark, 7
bottom, 9
branches, 9, 13
cones, 17, 19, 21
cracks, 7
evergreens, 15
groups, 13
leaves, 11

needles, 11, 13, 15, 21
parts, 17
scales, 17
seeds, 17, 19
top, 9
trunk, 5, 9
year, 15

Word Count: 138
Early-Intervention Level: 8

Editorial Credits
Martha E. Hillman, editor; Clay Schotzko/Icon Productions, cover designer; Sheri Gosewisch, photo researcher

Photo Credits
Dembinsky Photo Assoc. Inc./Adam Jones, cover; Darrell Gulin, 4; Randall B. Henne, 12
G. Alan Nelson, 6
Helen Longest-Slaughter, 20
Jack Glisson, 16
James P. Rowan, 1
Mark Turner, 10, 18
Unicorn Stock Photos/Betts Anderson, 8; Ted Rose, 14